"Soren's insights are both powerful and deeply meaningful. His unique ability to distill complex ideas into simple innovation frameworks and guidelines is inspiring to any organization."

—Alan Wolpert, General Manager,
Innovation North America, COLGATE-PALMOLIVE

"Soren's cross-industry examples, clear direction, and practical models help executives get their heads quickly wrapped around the role and importance of culture. Culture is the key to innovation, and *The Invisible Advantage* helps leaders assess, frame, and create a sustainable environment for both innovation and growth."

—Rebecca Romano, Vice President, Talent Development, NBCUNIVERSAL

"*The Invisible Advantage* captures the essence of what produces an entrepreneurial culture. Better yet, Soren provides practical tools that anyone can apply to their business, whether they're just starting out or leading an established organization."

—Glenn Allen, Cofounder, OPENTABLE

"Soren helped our leadership team assess, design, and build an action plan for further embedding innovation into our culture. His thoughtful models, tools, and highly collaborative approach created widespread engagement and alignment. Within just a few months, we've started to transform our structure, processes, and work environment in ways that will take our people, teams, and organization to the next level with new enthusiasm for innovative thinking and action."

—Kevin Martin, Chief Operating Officer,
KQED PUBLIC TELEVISION & RADIO, San Francisco

"In this entertaining and enlightening read, Soren makes the case that culture is your only lasting competitive advantage. Better yet, he reveals what it really takes to build an innovative culture."

—David Burkus, author of *Under New Management*

"Soren was fundamental in helping us jump-start our innovation program! His knowledge of the ideation and innovation process was paramount in leading a broad team of internal partners in understanding the nuance of offering up solutions to meet real-world problems. In *The Invisible Advantage*, Soren nails down the often-hidden success factors that lead to real, sustainable innovation."

—Alexis Edelstein, Trade Marketing Innovation, RED BULL

"*The Invisible Advantage* delivers on its promise. Working directly with Soren—using his questionnaire, interview guide, and frameworks—we rallied our globally disbursed organization to invest in innovation pilot projects, create innovation awards, sponsor idea competitions, and embrace an overall shift in our mindsets and culture."

—Jerry Yothment, General Manager, ARCELORMITTAL USA

"Soren Kaplan has helped our executive leaders participating in our Leadership Academy to understand and practice many of the principles and tools within *The Invisible Advantage*. The book simplifies a highly complex topic, using practical examples and a model so leaders and human resource practitioners can begin the process of understanding, and acting on, exactly what will inspire employees and make their culture more innovative."

—Herbert Vallier, Executive Vice President and
Chief Human Resources Officer, ASCENSION HEALTH

"Soren Kaplan's deep understanding of both innovation and organizational culture come together in a valuable framework with practical tools, which can be used by companies and executives to create an innovation culture, no matter what size organization or in what industry."

—Flemming Poulfelt, Professor and Vice Dean,
COPENHAGEN BUSINESS SCHOOL

"We all know innovation is essential for success. But how to actually get innovation requires a mix of art and science. The Invisible Advantage describes exactly what's needed to create a long-lasting culture of innovation."

—Michael Wiener, Global Business Leader, 3M HEALTH CARE

"Soren has a unique ability to simplify and distill vague topics like 'innovation' and 'culture' into practical strategies and tools. *The Invisible Advantage* can help anyone get their arms around how to actually lead the type of culture change that fosters innovation."

—David Underwood, Head of Talent Management and Analytics,
CSAA INSURANCE GROUP, a AAA Insurer

"Soren's dynamic style pulls his audience in, gets them processing, and challenges them to think differently. I have had the pleasure of seeing Soren swiftly engage leaders across industries and functions and scope; this book is another great example of his ability to help others drive real organizational change."

—Lacey Leone McLaughlin, Director, Executive Education,
CENTER FOR EFFECTIVE ORGANIZATIONS,
University of Southern California

"Competitive advantage is ultimately about culture, and aligning your organization's values, attitudes, and behaviors to strike a culture promoting innovation is precisely what The Invisible Advantage can help any leader achieve."

—Mark J. Laurie, PwC Managing Partner and
MELBOURNE BUSINESS SCHOOL PWC ASCENT PROGRAM

"Creating a culture of innovation can unlock the potential within your organization for a sustainable focus on meaningful innovation, whether it's the 'big disruptor' or the equally important incremental changes that 'add value now.' *The Invisible Advantage* shares real examples that demystify how to shape culture, enabling you to engage your entire team and achieve innovation from all corners of your organization."

—Dianne Auger, President,
ST. VINCENT'S MEDICAL CENTER FOUNDATION

"In *The Invisible Advantage*, Soren Kaplan's insight into what make organizations tick translates into a simple yet powerful structure that anyone can use to transform their culture to achieve more innovation. Every CEO should use this book as a guide to help promote innovation."

—Don Welsh, President and CEO,
DESTINATION MARKETING ASSOCIATION INTERNATIONAL

"In *The Invisible Advantage*, Soren Kaplan does a masterful job of uncovering the hidden success factors required to engage entire organizations in the creation of an innovation culture. Nonprofit organizations looking to shift their culture and expand their influence need to incorporate Soren's insights in order to create exceptional value for their members, communities, and the mission they serve."

—Scott Goudeseune, President and CEO,
AMERICAN COUNCIL ON EXERCISE

"Creating a culture of innovation is a tough task. *The Invisible Advantage* provides everything needed to assess, define, and shape the unique aspects of culture that promote real innovation. It's the only book I've seen that's actually a tool kit for culture change."

—Matt Tourdot, Vice President of Product Innovation
and Management, SPACESAVER CORPORATION

"*The Invisible Advantage* is far more than a book, it's a portal granting online access to a practical tool kit so powerful that it should be an indispensable guide for anyone charged with driving culture change in an organization."

—Matthew May, author of *Winning the Brain Game:*
Fixing the Seven Fatal Flaws of Thinking

The

INVISIBLE
ADVANTAGE

HOW TO CREATE A CULTURE OF INNOVATION

SOREN KAPLAN, PhD

GREENLEAF
BOOK GROUP PRESS

Published by Greenleaf Book Group Press
Austin, Texas
www.gbgpress.com

Distributed by Greenleaf Book Group

For ordering information or special discounts for bulk purchases, please contact Greenleaf Book Group at PO Box 91869, Austin, TX 78709, 512.891.6100.

Design and composition by Greenleaf Book Group
Cover design by Greenleaf Book Group

Cataloging-in-Publication data is available.

Print ISBN: 978-1-62634-321-4

eBook ISBN: 978-1-62634-322-1

Part of the Tree Neutral® program, which offsets the number of trees consumed in the production and printing of this book by taking proactive steps, such as planting trees in direct proportion to the number of trees used: www.treeneutral.com

Printed in China on acid-free paper

16 17 18 19 20 21   10 9 8 7 6 5 4 3 2

First Edition

CONTENTS

INTRODUCTION

Most of my clients want disruption—not *of* their business, but *for* their business. They want the revolutionary products, services, and business models that will transform both their organizations and their industries. Today, sustainable competitive advantage no longer exists. Products, services, technologies, and even business models come and go. They become commodities at an ever-faster pace. So what can we do?

The only defensible competitive advantage resides underneath the products, services, business processes, technologies, and business models we deliver to the world. It's generally invisible to your competitors, your partners, and even your own employees. It's your culture.

People have been talking about organizational culture for years. But most discussions haven't explicitly linked culture directly to innovation and business growth. Even fewer focus on the specific levers that directly influence innovation. This book does exactly that, revealing how your innovation culture can become your ultimate source of competitive advantage—your *invisible advantage*.

Culture is the collection of unwritten rules, norms, and values that influence people's behavior. When it comes to innovation, especially *disruptive innovation*, an organization's culture can be either the rocket fuel or death knell of an organization's ability to grow and thrive.

This book is about how to create a *culture of innovation—an environment that promotes freethinking, an entrepreneurial spirit, and sustainable value creation at all levels across all functions of an organization.*

The Invisible Advantage springboards off my award-winning book, *Leapfrogging*, by giving busy businesspeople exactly what they need—a strategic yet practical resource that's short and sweet. It's based on my more than twenty years of working across industries with CEOs of Fortune 500 companies, health-care organizations, and nonprofits. It taps into the extensive research and interviews I conducted in the course of writing *Leapfrogging*. And it addresses one of the most frequent questions my clients ask: How do you create a culture of innovation?

Here are today's realities that *The Invisible Advantage* tackles:

- **Competitive advantage is temporary.** Products, services, and even business models become commodities over time. If organizations do not continually invent and reinvent their competitive advantage, they risk being disrupted into obsolescence.

- **Culture is the only sustainable competitive advantage.** It's the invisible secret sauce that drives employee engagement, innovation, business growth, and continuous reinvention.

- **Every organization must unlock its innovation culture in its own unique way.** What works for Google and Apple might actually kill innovation in other companies. Effective best practices must be artfully adapted to the unique personality of your organization.

I often hear clients say, "We have plenty of ideas, but we just can't get traction with any of them." They're stuck, and here's the reason: Their company cultures stifle innovation.

The good news is that many leaders and organizations have finally recognized that real innovation and business growth don't result from just creating finely tuned processes, two-by-two matrices, or rigid business-planning templates.

The soft stuff is the hard stuff. That's why many companies overengineer the innovation process. They believe they need to squeeze out all aspects of uncertainty. What they don't realize is that uncertainty is one of the most essential ingredients of innovation. The trick is to avoid overstructuring what should be an organic process while also providing enough structure to consistently get organic results. The goal is to give just enough structure to help people navigate ambiguity and tap into the creative process without stifling it.

Organizations must also take a conscious look at the interplay of the other key factors that can stifle or support innovation. These include formal and informal leadership behaviors, organizational structure and processes, people's skills and talents, and formal and informal rewards and recognition.

This is what this book is about—revealing the specific success factors that must come together to promote real innovation. When the right variables align, great things can happen.

CHAPTER 1

SO YOU WANT TO BE A DISRUPTIVE INNOVATOR?

Be careful what you ask for. You might actually get it!

In today's buzzword-laden business world, we're enamored with the language *du jour*. Words and catchphrases like *lean in, enable, platform,* and, of course, *disruption* are all the rage. Given this book is about how to create a culture of innovation, I felt it necessary to dispel a few assumptions about disruptive innovation specifically, right out of the gate. These assumptions can impede our understanding of innovation itself—and how to shape culture around it—unless we put them into a broader context.

Why are so many of us looking for disruptive innovation? It's simple. Because we want the type of breakthroughs that transform industries, create new business models, and drive growth. Nothing wrong with that! But do we really want everyone in our organizations to be disruptive? No way.

Here's the issue: Although disruptive innovation is important, it isn't the only type of innovation that's necessary to survive, thrive, and win in today's rapidly changing world. Other types of innovation are equally essential. And you need everyone doing them.

The problem is that most companies either go for only the big bets or get stuck in a single-minded focus on the small stuff. If we only swing for the fences, we'll miss the opportunity to score on singles, doubles, or triples as well. And if we only go for the singles, we'll never win the Home Run Derby. The challenge is that we need a balanced approach, one that's focused on all types of innovation.

Disruptive Innovation's Dirty Secret

I believe it's important to understand the context of buzzwords, so we can fully appreciate both their value and their limitations. Let's start with a little story that goes back to the very source of disruptive innovation itself to understand today's state of innovation—and how we can rise above the buzz to create a true culture of innovation.

In 1998, when I was running the strategy group at Hewlett-Packard (HP), we invited Clayton Christensen, the iconic Harvard professor who wrote *The*

Innovator's Dilemma and coined the term disruptive innovation, to come speak to us.

We asked him a simple question, "How do you do disruptive innovation?"

Christensen shared compelling examples. He argued that companies, and entire industries, can be "disrupted" by unforeseen competitors—new entrants that offer up products or technologies at a fraction of the cost yet with equal or greater benefits compared to current options. The result? Customers abandon the old way and move to the new. Industry-leading companies die. New leaders arise. Wealth is destroyed and created all in the same breath. Disruption occurs.

Although I left HP a few years after that, Christensen's words stuck with me. Fast-forward to today—disruptive innovation is business's biggest paradigm. Just about everyone wants it or thinks they need it.

Disruptive innovation is an easily graspable concept, mostly because we've seen the recent casualties of disruption: Kodak, Blockbuster, Borders, Black-Berry. And most of us want to avoid a similar fate or, better yet, reap the benefits associated with being the disruptor, as Netflix, Amazon, and Apple have. Disruptive innovation—or avoiding its consequences—is now a widely embraced business imperative.

What most people don't realize is that there's a dirty little secret behind the concept, and that today's disruption frenzy has started to undermine the balanced approach that's needed to create a culture of innovation.

Old Idea, New Language

Few people know that the fundamental concept of disruptive innovation wasn't new when Christensen introduced it. In 1942 economist Joseph Schumpeter described the dynamics of "creative destruction," essentially the same thing as disruptive innovation.

Jump forward to 1994. The Massachusetts Institute of Technology's James Utterback published a groundbreaking book, *Mastering the Dynamics of Innovation*, which described how the ice-harvesting industry was displaced by "ice boxes" (a.k.a. refrigerators), how manual typewriters were stamped out by IBM's Selectric electric typewriter, and how something called electronic-imaging technology could pose a big threat to film-based photography in general and to Kodak in particular (it did).

All this was years before *The Innovator's Dilemma* made it onto the scene. What this previous research didn't have, however, was a catchy term like *disruptive* to tag onto the word *innovation*. The rest is history. Disruption is our lens.

Most people familiar with the research on innovation also know about paradigms. Paradigms are mental models that contain unquestioned assumptions about how things work. The world is flat. The sun revolves around the earth. These assumptions are accepted as truths, until they're turned upside down and replaced with an alternative paradigm. Paradigms have always existed, and they always will.

Just as *quality* and *reengineering* were the business world's lenses in the 1980s and 1990s, *disruptive innovation* is one of today's biggest paradigms.

While I'm in full agreement that disruptive innovation is a natural part of the evolution of organizations and industries, the "movement" has created a big problem for business. Here's the issue: *If we're overly concerned with disrupting or being disrupted, we neglect other types of innovation, innovation that can actually <u>lead</u> to disruption!* That's why we need everyone innovating—but doing it in a way that makes sense for their job function, which may mean simply focusing on process improvements, tweaks to current products, enhancing the customer experience, or anything else that may support today's business.

If Steve Jobs Didn't Try to Do It, Why Should You?

The reality is that most "disruptions" don't start out that way. Steve Jobs, arguably one of the greatest disruptive innovators of all time, said the same thing. "When we created the iTunes Music Store, we did that because we thought it would be great to be able to buy music electronically, not because we had plans to redefine the music industry."

Looking back, it's probably not too strong of a statement to say that Apple disrupted the music industry. But did Jobs know that's what he was doing at the time? No. Was it part of Apple's strategy? No. Apple created iTunes because it felt like the right thing to do to add value to customers and the world. Simple as that.

Take two other modern-day disruptors. Larry Page and Sergey Brin didn't start Google (now renamed Alphabet) with the intention of transforming the Internet, buying YouTube, or launching Android. Their very first step—and what kicked off their journey—was finding a way to more effectively prioritize library searches for academic research papers online. Yes, *library searches*. From there, they realized they could also index web pages. And, at first, they resisted including advertisements next to the search results. Good thing for them (and Alphabet shareholders), they changed their minds.

When we set our sights on creating a disruptive innovation, we can place unrealistic expectations on our organizations, employees, and ourselves. We lose sight of the realities that are inherent in the innovation process. It's like seeking fame for fame's sake versus simply having a great talent that leads to great performances, which then results in fame. It clouds our sense of what we're really doing.

If You Only Swing for the Fences, You Won't Score on Singles, Doubles, or Triples

The theory of disruptive innovation can indeed be helpful for understanding how technology has played a disruptive role in shaping the business and competitive landscape. But when this is your dominant lens and you're obsessed with hitting home runs (or being homered upon), you miss a lot of other opportunities to score. Just take Kodak, for example. About ten years before filing for bankruptcy in 2003, the company hired the head of HP's ink-jet printer business. This move was a "big bet" intended to help Kodak jump into the printer business as a response to rapidly falling 35-millimeter camera and film sales. The company took a single swing for the fences by trying to enter a billion-dollar industry and become the low-cost provider of both printers and ink—the classic disruptive-innovation strategy. It missed. Goodbye, Kodak.

Unlike disruptive innovations, incremental innovations are minor tweaks to existing products or services. Such innovations are fairly quick and easy to do; examples include new colors, flavors, features, benefits, or aspects of the customer experience. The principle behind *incremental innovation* is much more strategic and goes much deeper than the term suggests. Small tweaks, jelled with the right mindset and approach, oftentimes add up to bigger breakthroughs.

Dave Levin and Mike Feinberg, two former teachers with the Teach for America program, founded KIPP and created a network of a hundred inner-city charter schools with more than 27,000 students, and the schools are producing off-the-charts results. Just as Steve Jobs had wanted to do something *basic yet great* (i.e., to sell music electronically), so did Levin and Feinberg. They set out to create a school that truly works, and they built it through incremental innovation, one tweak at a time.

These two ex-teachers paint a simple slogan in the hallways of their schools: *There are no shortcuts*. School starts at 7:30 a.m. and ends at 5:00 p.m. Homework is usually about two hours per night. Teachers vow to make themselves available to any student at any time of day or night, and most students don't hesitate to call teachers at home for help, since teachers freely dole out their personal numbers. Kids attend school two Saturdays a month and the KIPP school year extends three weeks into the traditional summer break.

Nearly every KIPP school in the country is located in an inner-city neighborhood. More than nine out of ten KIPP students are Hispanic or African-American. Seven out of ten of them live below the poverty line. Most enter the program performing well below grade level. Typically, less than ten percent of children with such backgrounds go on to finish college. KIPP students boast a ninety percent graduation rate—not from high school, *from college*. All this through hard work, determination, and incremental innovation.

Between incremental and disruptive innovation lies sustaining innovation. Sustaining innovations aren't necessarily about big bets. But they're not about little tweaks either. Sustaining innovations involve trying something that feels like a bit of a stretch and then seeing what happens. If they work, they can "sustain" the business (and ideally grow it) into the long term. Sometimes they flop. But, now and then, they go big. When they do, sometimes the storytellers look back and call them disruptive.

Taco Bell's Doritos Locos Taco is a taco with a giant Dorito tortilla chip as its shell. Sound crazy? In the taco's first ten weeks on the market, Taco Bell sold a hundred million of them. To date, Taco Bell has sold more than half a billion, generated more than $1 billion in sales, and has had its new product called the most successful fast-food menu item of all time. The Doritos Locos Taco wasn't meant to "disrupt" the traditional taco. And it didn't involve just an incremental tweak, such as adding a new spice to the taco meat either. It was a decent-sized experiment that took a great deal of effort and that expanded the definition of *taco* for the world. And like most things that, in retrospect, look a lot like disruptive innovations (especially to McDonald's and Burger King), its success surprised even the person at Taco Bell who developed and introduced it, Steve Gomez, who admitted, "I was blown away with how immediately popular Doritos Locos Tacos became."

Another company that has steered clear of disruptive innovation by going after modest-sized opportunities is Fujifilm. Fifteen years ago, the company stood at the same starting line as Kodak. Today, Kodak is bankrupt while Fujifilm has a $20 billion market cap. We don't think about Fujifilm as a disruptive innovator. It isn't. But by most measures of success, it has weathered the storm and come out the other end quite successfully. The company has continued the march toward adapting to the digital world by getting into 3-D photography. They've entered dozens of new businesses, ranging from television cameras to medical products to thin-film packaging for candy. Disruptive innovations? No. Sustaining innovation was the savior—and the company's growth engine.

In today's innovation-obsessed world, disruption encapsulates the holy grail. Incremental and sustaining innovations are the all-too-often overlooked steps that lead you to the grail. The original theory of disruptive innovation is fundamentally about technologies and products. The real world rewards those who build new business models, extend brands, create new channels, find new markets, redesign customer experiences, reinvent business processes, and do the other work that most seasoned innovators know truly shapes the future.

And that's what creating a culture of innovation is all about. Yes, such a culture can lead to the disruptive stuff, but it can also foster other types of innovation—which are equally necessary for improving today's business and adding value in everything you do, all while you're trying to transform the future.

Innovation culture is the new competitive advantage—or your Achilles heel.

CHAPTER 2

THE INVISIBLE ADVANTAGE

The soft stuff is the hardest stuff for competitors to copy.

Most people become intimately familiar with the concept of culture when they travel abroad. They experience unfamiliar customs, food, music, art, language, and attitudes. If you've ever been to Paris and ended up waiting forever for the check in a French restaurant, you may know what I mean—the unwritten rule is that you have to proactively ask for the check at the end of a meal, otherwise you'll never get it! Why? There's a shared value in French culture that meals should be enjoyed and contribute to one's joie de vivre. Even the stereotypically snippy French waiters respect this norm, so it's up to you to decide when you're finished and ready to turn over your table to the next guest (quite the opposite of customers' experience at many bustling American restaurants).

Just as countries have cultures, so do geographic regions, organizations, and subgroups and teams within organizations. When I work with my clients, I often find that starting with a slightly bigger picture of culture can help clarify what many people see as an ambiguous concept.

Silicon Valley's Innovation Culture

Let's start with Silicon Valley—a place where I've both lived and worked—as an example of innovation culture. Mark Zuckerberg moved Facebook from his Harvard dorm room to "the Valley." Steve Jobs grew up there. The stereotypical image of the entrepreneurial garage comes from the real one in Palo Alto that housed HP.

Other regions and countries have tried to replicate it. But Silicon Valley's unique culture makes it a global innovation powerhouse that can't be copied over to other eager cities, states, or countries. What's happening in the Valley provides a great example of how norms, values, and behavior all merge to reinforce innovation.

Smart people stream into the Valley from Stanford, the University of California at Berkeley, and other Bay Area universities. Venture capitalists sprinkle funding across the most promising start-ups. Companies collaborate while competing. Experienced employees remain on the never-ending lookout for their next big opportunity—and frequently jump jobs across industries and markets, even to competitors. Silicon Valley's fertile ground—which literally started out as farmland—has become the ultimate fertilizer for growing some of the most innovative companies in the world.

In a recent discussion I had with a senior executive at Netflix, for example, I asked if the company had an innovation strategy. He gave me a little puzzled expression and said that Netflix itself is a disruptive innovation. Innovation is so embedded in the company's culture that it doesn't need a specific strategy to make it happen. It *is* innovation.

As a result of the region's inherently innovative environment, entrepreneurs make the pilgrimage to set up shop in the Valley. Established companies like Comcast and Wal-Mart plunk down their new ventures here. Even the governments of countries like Denmark, Finland, and Ireland have established incubators to help their compatriots from home tap into the secrets of Silicon Valley culture.

On any given day, one can find dozens of networking breakfasts, lunchtime speakers, and after-work cocktail parties, creating a way for people to connect. Many Silicon Valley companies use similar principles to promote this kind of environment internally. They know that cubicles create barriers, so they quite literally tear down the walls. Facebook, for example, frequently reorganizes its office space to mix up people and teams. And Google even provides office space within its buildings to start-ups it believes possess big potential.

Hung all around its offices, Facebook's pervasive and provocative posters, for example, promote the fact that "done is better than perfect" and that everyone should "move fast and break things." Like Facebook, most Silicon Valley companies value trial and error, realizing it's better to put ideas forward in their infancy than wait until they're fully baked. The goal is to quickly learn what works, what doesn't, and go from there. It's better to sacrifice saving face and instead save time and money.

Many Silicon Valley–based companies formulate innovation strategies to support their business strategies. Others, like Netflix, view their entire business as the disruptive innovation. Whatever the approach, these companies have big visions focused on making the biggest possible difference for their customers.

Many established companies create "innovation departments" to incubate the next big idea. That can help, but creating a culture of innovation comes from building a broader environment in which all employees clearly see their role in adding real value. One of the most telling anecdotes illustrating why this is so critically important comes from a quote from Tim Cook, Apple's CEO, addressing how the company goes about innovating: "There's no formula," Cook exclaimed. "If there was a formula, a lot of companies would have bought their ability to innovate." Cook's quote is actually quite stunning. Apple, arguably one of the most innovative companies in the world, says there's no formula for the innovation process!

The Invisible Advantage

In actuality, Apple does have a formula of sorts. And so do many other companies that know how to drive innovation and competitive differentiation. The formula is to promote and foster a work environment where everyone knows his or her unique role in "changing the game" for the better, no matter what the individual's job role or function is.

There's a lot going on in Silicon Valley that flies under the radar of most people's awareness. It's not much different from the proverbial question about whether fish know they live in water (my hunch is that they don't). It's really not that difficult to decipher your innovation culture by looking at leadership behavior, organizational structure, business processes, metrics and incentives, rewards and recognition, and the stories and symbols that reinforce (or inhibit) innovation. By understanding the things that shape norms, values, and behavior, it becomes possible to influence them—*and to create a culture of innovation.*

Savvy leaders both inside and outside Silicon Valley shape the cultures of their companies to drive innovation. They know that culture—the values, norms, unconscious messages, and subtle behaviors of leaders and employees—often limits performance. These invisible forces are responsible for the fact that seventy percent of all organizational change efforts fail. The trick? Design the interplay between the company's explicit strategies with the way you want people to relate to one another and to the organization.

Just as Apple's Tim Cook inferred, there's no formula, and there really are an unlimited number of ways to create a culture of innovation. But the good news is that there are some key principles and practices. The next five chapters provide specific strategies for influencing the soft stuff to promote innovation and business growth. What you'll see is that successful innovation cultures overcome the pervasive risk-avoidance that plagues many organizations. The leaders who have fostered these cultures know that the *safe* bet is actually the *unsafe* bet.

As counterintuitive as it may seem, promoting innovation is not the same as promoting risk taking! With a true culture of innovation, people don't feel like innovation results from taking risks per se, but rather from creativity and learning. Many of my clients ask me how they can promote risk taking. What they don't realize is that they're asking the wrong question. The goal is to eliminate the feeling of risk altogether.

The rest of this book shows you how.

Frame the way you want
to change the world,
and make your intentions
about the customer.

CHAPTER 3

BE INTENTIONAL WITH YOUR INNOVATION INTENT

Define what you want. Then (re)shape assumptions around it.

Most corporate visions and missions sound alarmingly alike: Become the number one provider of blah, blah, blah. These generic, broad-based goals might rev up sales teams, but they do little to spark ingenuity. Perhaps the worst thing a company can do is give "innovation marching orders" without any guideposts. That's when the focus gets lost, teams spin their wheels, and innovation culture gets crushed.

Create Your Innovation Intent

Here's the goal: *Frame the way you want to change the world, and make it about the customer.* For example, the software company Intuit—the developer of Quicken,

QuickBooks, and TurboTax—makes its mission abundantly clear: "To improve our customers' financial lives so profoundly they can't imagine going back to the old way." The public television and radio station in San Francisco, KQED, describes its innovation intent a bit more broadly: "Doing the right thing for our audience, the community, our staff, and our organization by continually assessing, prioritizing, and improving what we do and how we do it." KQED anchors its innovation intent in a set of "innovation operating principles" that operationalize its definition of innovation. Hung around the building in the form of posters, KQED's innovation intent and operating principles provide a reminder of what's important when it comes to innovation, each and every day.

I recently had the opportunity to meet with the executive team of a leading energy company in Australia. I shared the ideas behind having an innovation intent. After I finished, one of the executives scratched his head and said, "We have an innovation intent, but it's about how we exist to create shareholder value." He went on to conclude, "I guess we should focus a bit more on the customer."

Heck yeah was all I could think (though I didn't say exactly that in response to him). I did respond by saying that few people are truly motivated to get up in the morning to help shareholders increase value. Increasing shareholder value might be the *result* of innovation, but it's not what motivates most people to give it their all over the long term.

KQED

INNOVATION
Operating Principles

Innovation at KQED
Doing the right thing for our audience, the community, supporters, our staff, and our organization by continually assessing, prioritizing, and improving what we do and how we do it.

Make strategic decisions | Connect our actions to the strategic plan and organizational priorities

Continually assess how we work | Find new ways to allocate and focus resources to maximize capacity

Build efficient processes | Apply methods and processes that are not single person-dependent

Apply technology | Leverage technology to improve what we do and how we do it, and to eliminate as much paper wherever possible

Focus on speed | Move quickly with intention and without compromising quality

27

An innovation intent should focus on making a big difference for those you serve. Trying to create positive change in the world for your customers, each and every day, is a much better motivator.

Having an innovation intent is critically important for gaining focus. Without a grounding in your specific business, the definition of innovation for the organization remains too open to broad interpretation. It's one thing to tell people to "go innovate." It's another to tell people you want specific types of innovation that deliver measurable results.

Define and Communicate Your Innovation Portfolio Strategy

The CSAA Insurance Group, one of the insurance companies associated with the American Automobile Association, uses three types of innovation to help its 3,800 employees understand their role in fostering a culture of insight and innovation. The model includes distinctions between incremental, sustaining, and disruptive innovation, just as I previously described. Leaders at the CSAA Insurance Group are also quite realistic in that they expect the vast majority of the company's innovation to be incremental. It's perfectly OK that most people focus on smaller tweaks and improvements to business processes, the company website, or how seamlessly customers can file and receive payments for claims. All of that is the company's core business, and having the majority of people striving to improve the core business every day is indeed recognized as a culture of innovation. But the organization's model also includes next-generation sustaining innovation and the even bigger disruptive possibility that it may need to consider reinventing its core auto insurance business in the longer term. Fewer overall resources are focused on these bigger efforts than running the core business and that's also OK, since the company is funding the future from current operations and taking a portfolio approach to innovation.

Here's a simple model that any organization can apply to tee up its definition of *innovation* and take a portfolio approach to allocating its time and effort:

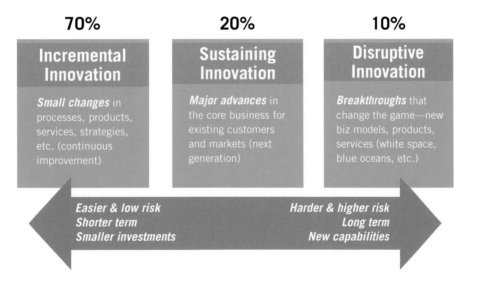

Connecting your innovation intent to all three types of innovation helps link innovation to both the current and future direction of the organization. It demystifies the whole concept of innovation, which can be fairly amorphous for those outside the executive suite (and sometimes even within the executive suite), molding the idea into something concrete.

Every Function Should Have Its Own Definition of Innovation

An innovation intent isn't limited to just the company. Each and every business function can also have its own innovation intent. This is critically important, since not everyone interacts with external customers. Some groups might support internal customers—other functions or groups in the organization. Innovating how to serve internal customers is just as important, because making those groups more effective can ultimately have a positive impact on the external customer.

I hear similar statements from executives within internal support functions that sound like this: "My company says that innovation is a strategic imperative, but I'm in HR and I have no idea what that means for me." I could easily substitute "HR" with "IT" or "Legal" or "Finance." These shared support functions often struggle to translate their company's innovation imperatives—which they assume are always oriented toward new product or service development for customers. With an innovation intent at the functional level, it becomes possible to rally an entire department around creating new forms of value. Here are some examples of innovation intent statements that can do just that:

- **Finance:** To deliver financial insight that drives strategic business decisions, new market opportunities, and the innovation process

- **HR:** To recruit and grow top talent that shapes the future of our company and that transforms the industry

- **IT:** To provide tools and services that deliver insight for employees and that accelerate innovation and optimize the customer experience

An intentional, specific innovation intent helps people see how innovation connects to what they do and how they do it. For some, innovation may result from incremental process improvements. For others, it may involve designing the next generation of products and services. There's no one right answer, but everyone should view the importance and relevance of innovation through a unique, individual lens.

How Innovation Intent Shapes Culture

Without the focus an innovation intent provides, people tend to think innovation belongs to someone else (such as Research and Development) and assume it isn't part of their job. Lack of a thoughtfully defined innovation intent also makes it difficult for leaders to create specific programs, processes, metrics, and rewards that shape values and behavior, because specific expectations and measures of success usually aren't clear beyond the call for "more ideas."

And it gets worse. Sometimes leadership says it wants a culture of innovation and then makes innovation a business imperative but leaves results open to happenstance. Vague directives of this kind can actually have the opposite effect on the company's culture. There's nothing worse than saying the organization has an imperative for innovation and then doing nothing to back it up. Innovation then becomes lip service, since people's experiences don't change one bit, which embeds *innovation passivity* into the culture—exactly the opposite of what you want.

Here's a simple model that outlines why people and organizations get stuck and what leaders need to do to unstick things.

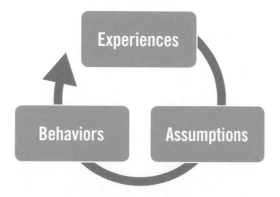

Here's how this plays out in real life at a very basic level. When I was seven years old, two big German shepherds knocked me to the ground as I was walking to school. The experience scared the daylights out of me. I went running home in tears. From then on, anytime I saw a big dog, I would become overwhelmed with fear and would do everything I could to avoid it no matter where I was—on the street, in the park, or at a friend's home. My unfortunate experience led to an assumption about all dogs (that they were dangerous), which in turn shaped my fear-based "irrational" behavior (running away in terror). It wasn't until I was in my teens and my family adopted our first dog that I was able to break this long-standing assumption-belief-behavior cycle. The new experience of pet ownership started to chip away at my assumptions and beliefs. *Hey, this dog is nice. It's not knocking me over! It's not scaring me!* Eventually I overcame my visceral fear and started behaving differently. Today, I no longer cower in the corner when visiting friends with big dogs!

The same dynamics exist in organizations. They might not be as obvious (and physically scary) as a big, slobbery German shepherd, but they can create just as much havoc. Leaders do things, consciously or unconsciously, that shape the experiences of those around them. Those experiences drive assumptions, which influence behavior.

Want new behavior that leads to innovation? First, put a stake in the ground regarding your innovation intent. Leaders at Intuit did just that when they said they wanted to "improve our customers' financial lives so profoundly they can't imagine going back to the old way." But Intuit went one step further, to the second step, and reinforced its innovation intent with some very specific employee experiences. For example, the company physically brings customers into its offices to mix things up. Intuit's monthly "customer office hours" provide all employees, from the software engineer to the HR manager to the financial analyst, with the opportunity to see, hear, and talk to real live customers. The focus is on bringing customers—including their needs, desires, and pain points—directly into the organization. There's no formal agenda. Some employees just listen. Others test assumptions and ideas for new products and services. Intuit is a great example of a company that designs employee experiences that are directly connected to its innovation intent.

Another example is *Sequence*, a digital brand and product agency in San Francisco. Every month, the company surprises employees with "boomerang passes," named after an Australian airline promotion for dirt-cheap, same-day round-trip flights to surprise destinations. The company randomly gives the boomerang pass to one lucky employee each month. Upon arriving in the office, the recipient is whisked away on a one-day adventure. Past excursions have included Segway tours of redwood forests, horseback riding, flower-arranging classes, trapeze lessons, and a trip to Las Vegas for a tour of Zappos. Sequence recognizes that inspiration and growth come from stretching oneself through new experiences. Employees return to share insights about how seemingly unrelated adventures inform—and could potentially transform—the business. These employee experiences reinforce the company's belief that in a world of growing commoditization, it's the quality of the customer experience that creates differentiation, something *Sequence* strives to bring to everything it does.

These are just a few of the numerous examples that show how specific structures, processes, and tools create new experiences for people—experiences focused on challenging the status quo, trying new things, and adding value. In the following chapters, you'll get more practical examples of what you can do to create and inspire others through delivering different types of experiences that foster a culture of innovation.

Awesome Example!

Zipcar

Orchestrating Experiences to Remake Assumptions

I recently had the opportunity to do a little work with Andrew Daley, the vice president of Member Acquisition for Zipcar. Zipcar's unique approach to creating a membership model for car sharing almost single-handedly established the "sharing economy" in the United States and paved the way for business models like those of Uber and Airbnb.

Zipcar members aren't like the rest of the crowd—most are under thirty-five years old (also known as the millennial generation) and view car ownership a bit differently from the mainstream. Faced with high student-loan bills and diminished opportunities to land high-paying jobs, many millennials believe cars are too expensive for them to own, especially after taking into account the costs of insurance, gas, and parking.

Zipcar's low-cost annual membership gives its 900,000 members access to its fleet of vehicles stationed across numerous locations around 470 cities. Unlike traditional rental car companies, members can take cars out for an hour or a day, and gas and insurance are included. Simple.

But even a business model innovator like Zipcar must eventually respond to a changing world. Modern day millennials are radically different from those of ten years ago, when Zipcar revved up its start-up engine. Today's millennials, for example, live and die by their mobile phones. In fact, according to Zipcar's research, almost half of all millennials believe that losing their phone would be a bigger hardship than losing access to a car! And the majority believes losing their phone would be a greater tragedy (so to speak) than losing access to a desktop computer, laptop, or a TV.

So, here's the stark reality that recently crept up on Zipcar: It had designed its entire customer experience as an online experience and didn't have a way to sign up, service, and help members manage their memberships from their phones. The world had changed and Zipcar needed to change its operating model along with it. This wouldn't necessarily require a big shift in customers' behavior, since they were already mobile savvy. It would, however, require a big shift in employee mindsets and behavior, and Zipcar needed to move fast.

Zipcar did two things to jump-start its new mobile model. First, the company brought the new breed of customer to its office to give employees a taste of the twenty-first century's mobile reality. Zipcar's "member roundtables" occur on Saturdays and include about a dozen customers who share their needs, experiences, wishes, and feedback directly with the Zipcar staff. Roundtables are undeniable experiences—it's hard to disregard customer needs after a face-to-face conversation. These types of direct interactions with customers, whether at Zipcar or elsewhere, are powerful ways to shift employee mindsets and create the impetus for change.

Zipcar also orchestrated a different type of employee experience, one that would immediately become a symbol of its new "mobile first" strategic mindset. Employees were invited to a meeting where leadership discussed its new mobile business imperative. To help drive home the point, people were given sledgehammers so they could personally take up arms against the "old view" by taking turns pounding on two old desktop computers. Smashing the old to bring in the new (literally and figuratively) created a poignant experience and instantly wrote corporate folklore that could be passed on as a symbol of exactly what's needed for the future.

Carving out time for innovation doesn't have to mean radically remaking the corporate time clock.

CHAPTER 4

STEP IN—
THEN STEP BACK

Create a structure for unstructured innovation.

I've delivered keynotes and workshops to thousands of people worldwide. No matter where I go, people inevitably lament that they just don't have time to innovate. Apparently they're just too busy running today's business to think about what they're going to do in the future. Here's the painful reality: Time is a critical ingredient for innovation (sad, but true!).

Time Is the Fuel of Innovation

Giving up control when the pressure is greatest is the ultimate innovation paradox. That's why iconic brands like 3M and Google allocate between ten and twenty percent of employees' work hours as "free time," during which employees experiment with new ideas. The software company Atlassian encourages employees to take "FedEx Days"—paid days off to work on any problem they want. But there's a catch: Like FedEx, they must deliver something of value twenty-four hours later.

If you don't make time for innovation, you won't get it. It's a simple truth of innovation. So, arguably, leadership's number one job is to make sure everyone sees innovation as his or her job. And giving or creating time for it goes a long way. The goal is to create a structure for unstructured time.

To be clear, carving out time for innovation doesn't have to mean radically remaking the corporate time clock. Simply setting aside twenty minutes in a weekly meeting to explore "new ideas for making things better" can be enough to start a cultural shift in many organizations. But, of course, something must be done with those ideas. Otherwise, instead of taking a step forward, the culture may ultimately take a giant leap backward.

Leaders at companies like Intuit use time as a reward because they believe it's the biggest motivator of corporate intrapreneurs. Intuit recognizes innovations each year by displaying them on the Innovation Wall of Fame at their corporate office. The company also gives its best business innovators three months of "unstructured" time, which can be used in one big chunk or spread out over six months, for part-time exploration of new opportunities. Using time wisely creates a major incentive to get more time to play with.

If Time Is Fuel, a Toolkit Is the Car

Time in itself isn't sufficient to create a culture of innovation. It's also important to show people how to innovate. Providing toolkits, or a structure for new thinking and experimentation, helps people embrace the creative process and encourages them to join in. There are some pretty good off-the-shelf tools that can help build employee skill sets. Some of the best are available free, such as the Stanford Design School's Bootcamp Bootleg. Intuit applied the design thinking underlying Stanford's model to create its Catalyst Toolkit, a guide that was made available to all employees and the public and that includes self-serve ingredients for cooking up innovation.

There are many toolkit and innovation processes out there. All of them share various features, including a model, step-by-step process, and specific tools that can be used within their various steps. The model and tools are one thing, embedding the toolkit into the culture is another.

Intuit branded their toolkit by calling it the "Catalyst Toolkit." The software company Adobe has their own, which they've named Kickbox. Giving your model and toolkit an identity can help infuse it into the culture by giving people a symbol for innovation.

Whatever the format, "toolkits" give people guidance and structure to navigate the inherently ambiguous innovation process. Couple toolkits with time to create a context ripe for innovation.

Adobe's Kickbox
Big Ideas Come in Small Boxes

There's a big buzz going on about a little box. In the world of business innovation, Adobe's Kickbox is being billed as one of the best do-it-yourself innovation toolkits. I had a chance to catch up with Mark Randall, the chief strategist and vice president of creativity at Adobe, who's the mind behind this culture-shaping strategy.

When Mark joined Adobe, he was asked to use his experience to teach others how to innovate. With his history in building start-ups, he wondered if it was possible to establish the same type of innovative environment within a large corporation.

"One of the things that many big companies struggle with is sustaining the creative mindset throughout the organization," Mark says. "Innovation is a pursuit that comes from inside. People naturally want

to innovate. If you spend any time watching your kids at play, you see them creating and finding new imaginative solutions. It's like Picasso said, 'Every child is an artist. The problem is remaining an artist as we grow up.'"

Mark's quote from Picasso captures an even bigger issue at play. Consider a start-up as being in its infancy—where organizational culture is being born—compared to a large, established company, where "how things are done" is well established. The problem of the established company is the same as that of the adult artist: how to remain creative despite maturity. And that's exactly why Mark created Kickbox.

Developing Kickbox was an attempt to unleash latent creativity from across the entire organization. As Mark describes it, the goal of Kickbox is to systematically "remove the barriers that suppress innovative behavior." In most companies, employees share ideas and then corporate executives decide the ideas' fate. The problem is that the ideas have to be perfect out of the gate and really never have a chance to evolve through trial and error. Such a system is the opposite of how things work in start-ups, where testing, learning, and fast failures are part of the culture.

The Kickbox program gives employees the tools and freedom to take their ideas straight to customers for testing. It's a compelling concept, but here's where it gets even more radical: Employees are given a little red box—the Kickbox—that includes a $1,000 prepaid credit card to be used to test their idea. No strings are attached: no receipts, no expense reporting, and no questions asked.

There's really only one prerequisite. To get the Kickbox, employees must sign up for a workshop that includes training in Adobe's six-step innovation process. According to Mark, "the power to act and to innovate is in the hands of the participants, and each idea takes on a unique life of its own." The six levels of Kickbox's self-directed process include Inception, Ideate, Improve, Investigate, Iterate, and Infiltrate.

As part of the Investigate step, employees are taught how to put their $1,000 to work, usually through learning how to place online ads to see if potential customers understand the idea and are interested enough to click through. Ad links go to a test website, which further describes the value proposition of the not-yet-existent product. To keep responses from being skewed by Adobe's well-known brand, the ads, product descriptions, and websites don't feature the Adobe brand.

If employees manage to complete all six levels within the red box, they receive another box—this time blue—with instructions and support that help them move their idea toward a real product or service. But this time there's no cash. The merit of the idea has to sell itself. To graduate

Start

The red box contains six levels, each with objectives called actions. Complete these actions to advance to the next level. Once you begin, the red box can only be exited by succeeding or by giving up. Here is the secret to beating the red box: don't give up.

If you conquer the red box, you earn an exceptional prize: a blue box. What awaits you in the blue box? There is only one way to find out.

[Begin]

Inception. 1 — To start any journey without understanding your true purpose is to fail before you begin. Your own motivations illuminate the path to success.

Ideate. 2 — Great ideas emerge from great insight. Learn to spark your imagination by observing the world not as it is - but as it should be.

Improve. 3 — All ideas begin life as bad ideas. Learn to grow bad ideas into good ideas and the secret of knowing which is which.

Investigate. 4 — Is an idea valuable? It's a question only customers can answer. Find out quickly by validating your ideas with real-world experiments.

Iterate. 5 — Assess the data from your experiments to evolve your hypotheses. Devise clever experiments to reveal the true nature of your idea.

Infiltrate. 6 — Even great ideas must prove their worth in corporate combat. To conquer the red box, use data to sell an idea to your organization.

[Stop. Rest.]

Collect your blue box. Change the world.

beyond the red box, the idea must earn early funding support from a manager or executive, ensuring the next iteration of the opportunity is fully anchored in adding value to the business.

Here's the final Kickbox kicker. Adobe has open-sourced Kickbox, so the entire toolkit is available for download (though you'll need to provide the $1,000 prepaid credit card yourself). You can get Kickbox on Adobe's website.

If you're not measuring how far you've come, you won't know if you're getting closer to where you want to be.

CHAPTER 5

MEASURE WHAT'S MEANINGFUL

Decide what you want. Then measure it.

Management guru Peter Drucker once said, "What's measured improves." In other words, you get what you measure. For many companies, coming up with ideas often isn't the problem. The challenge is turning ideas into something real that delivers an impact. This is where metrics can make the difference between no ideas, lots of ideas that go nowhere, and real innovation.

So, what metrics should you use? The first step involves figuring out *what* to measure. In its early days, Facebook measured how often its users returned to its site. Everything Facebook did focused on blowing out this single metric. Open-Table, the restaurant reservation service, focused on two metrics that allowed it to become the dominant player: growing the numbers of restaurants in its network and increasing the number of consumers making reservations.

Customer-oriented numbers are clearly essential. But other indicators can drive internal innovation, too. After Procter and Gamble realized that outside partnerships were an important driver of market breakthroughs, the company decided to measure (and increase) the percentage of new products that used breakthrough technologies from partners. Externally driven innovation jumped from ten percent to more than fifty percent and resulted in new products, including Mr. Clean Magic Erasers and Tide Pods.

Metrics are a combination of art and science. In today's innovation-obsessed world that's so hooked on data analytics and finding metrics for anything and everything, it's a bit ironic that there's no standardized way to measure innovation itself.

Arguably, one of leadership's most important roles is to set strategic goals and then measure and promote their progress. The trick is to inspire action around the goals you set. According to the consulting firm McKinsey, more than seventy percent of corporate leaders tout innovation as one of their top three business priorities, but only twenty-two percent set innovation-performance metrics. It's hard to believe that in the age of data analytics, so many executive teams would allow this "innovation-metrics gap" to exist.

Why aren't more companies measuring innovation? Because, like the concept of culture, innovation is a nebulous topic. Definitions differ. Expectations vary.

Garbage In, Garbage Out. Nothing In, Nothing Out.

If you believe in the age old adage "garbage in, garbage out," then the scope of the problem becomes painfully poignant. This similar maxim also holds true: Nothing in, nothing out. If you don't measure innovation, are you still getting it? Certainly not in any systematic way.

Some might argue that the very act of measuring anything creative stifles such efforts out of the gate or that innovation is just plain impossible to quantify. They're wrong. More important is this question: Do you really want to leave the future up to creative chance? It's not exactly a viable strategy.

Measuring innovation is a combination of art and science, which is precisely why it's tough to do. If you go too far—as 3M did when it applied the rigorous Six Sigma model to its creative process—you might actually get less of what you really want.

The most innovative organizations carefully consider both what goes into the innovation process and what should come out of it. They focus on different types of measurements and include both the quantitative side of the business (hard numbers) and the qualitative side (such as leadership behavior).

Articulate the Endgame: Define the Outputs

Most companies understandably zero in on top line revenue and overall profitability when it comes to gauging success. Many also focus on their net promoter scores. These high-altitude metrics are indeed important, but they have limited value for measuring—and driving—innovation. Why? They're numbers. They don't take into account what people want. More important, they don't inspire action toward specific goals.

The objective is to disrupt the business-as-usual mindset. From a quantitative perspective, here are some metrics you can use as springboards for potential innovation:

- Percentage of revenue or profit coming from international versus domestic markets

- Revenues from new products or services introduced in the past X year(s)

- Revenues from products or services sold to new customer segments

- Percentage of existing customers that trade up to next-generation products or services

- Percentage of revenue coming from services versus products (or vice versa)

- Royalty or licensing revenue from intellectual property

Innovation-savvy organizations frame their endgames around goals derived from these sorts of metrics. They use them to identify potential opportunities and to guide their progress. That way, the value of the innovation isn't tied to some dreamy notion of "creativity." It's tied to very real (and quantifiable) outcomes. To repeat Peter Drucker's excellent quote, "What's measured improves." Said another way, if you're not measuring how far you've come, you won't know if you're getting any closer to where you want to be.

Fuel the Innovation Engine: Define the Inputs.

Measuring innovation also involves setting specific goals that will help fuel the process—the things you do internally to help you hit your targets. When you give people targets, they take on responsibility for hitting them. And in the process, they produce experiences and success stories that then reinforce more experiences. The goal is to jump-start this kind of positive feedback loop.

Lots of companies have used carefully calculated strategies to create cultures of innovation. They establish measures that explicitly promote certain behaviors. They shape their environments so people have enough time, resources, and focus to turn the creative process into real value creation. Measuring the inputs helps take the lip service out of it.

Coca-Cola's Venturing and Emerging Brands (VEB) group, for example, has a big charter: to create Coke's next billion-dollar brands. Coke leadership knew that if the company wanted to get big outputs, it needed different inputs. That's why it created VEB. Coke sponsors VEB teams to use unconventional methods that include "an amalgamation of science, art and serendipity" to uncover and meet emerging customer needs in the beverage world. Employees within VEB are given money, resources, and time to explore major opportunities. It's paying off. Brands they've acquired and built up include Fuze juice drinks, Illy Issimo ready-to-drink coffee, Honest Tea, and Zico coconut water.

General Electric takes a different approach. Over the past decade, employees have filed more than 20,000 patents, many of which are paving the way for the company to assume a leadership position in sustainable energy and the "industrial Internet." The emphasis on protecting intellectual property runs deep in the company's culture and started when GE's founder established the company's research and development function in the early 1900s. GE has always viewed patents as an essential input to innovation. Its recent partnership with the product-innovation social network Quirky—which makes GE's patent portfolio available to the Quirky community—shows that it is serious about carrying that tradition into the future.

One reason the innovation-metric gap exists is that what works for one company might be too fuzzy for the next. There aren't any metrics standards. That said, there are a few things you can measure in order to figure out how innovative your company's culture is. This measurement is also the first step in figuring out how to reshape that culture and promote new behaviors.

Leadership

- Percentage of funding for game changers versus small tweaks to existing products or services

- Percentage of senior executives' time that is focused on the future versus on daily operations

- Percentage of new innovations that come from external sources, such as partnerships, crowdsourcing, or open innovation

Employees

- Number of ideas turned into patents by employees

- Number of ideas turned into innovation experiments by employees

- Number of teams that submit projects for innovation awards

- Percentage of employees trained in the innovation process

Customers

- Number of ideas submitted by customers through "open innovation" programs

- Number of new product or service ideas that come from mining social networks

- Number of customers that help test and refine new ideas

Pick a few of these to create your own metrics mash-up. The optimal mash-up promotes very specific actions and behaviors, not generalized ones.

Here's another reason for the innovation-metrics gap: Finding the right things to measure is a process in itself. And it's hard. Every company has its own organizational culture, so every company must fine-tune what it measures to reinforce the goals, values, and norms that it finds critical for inspiring innovation (and best practices around innovation). Still, without metrics, you're rolling the dice. At best, your default strategy is little more than "something in, something out." That's not a whole lot better than "garbage in, garbage out."

Yum! Brands

Quantifying Innovation to Drive Business Growth

Yum! Brands, owner of the fast-food chains Pizza Hut and KFC (a.k.a. Kentucky Fried Chicken), had stopped growing. The U.S. market just wasn't consuming greasy takeout at levels that would make shareholders continue to smile. The company recognized it couldn't get a big enough jolt by simply tweaking its supply chain or through standard efficiency measures. It needed a big change.

Leaders at Yum! Brands decided to expand into foreign markets. They set a quantifiable goal—*to increase the overall proportion of the company's international revenue*—which they knew would require a fundamentally different approach.

Like many global companies, Yum! Brands set its sights on the big kahuna: China. The company's strategists were smart from the outset.

They recognized that what worked in the United States would be sure to fail in such a radically different market as China.

In a country where finger-lickin'-good fried chicken was about as foreign as apple pie, the company had little choice but to explore unfamiliar customer needs, test out new products, and build new business models. Rather than merely replicating what KFC already did well, the company decided to take a step back and study what Chinese customers wanted.

As a result of this new approach, KFC introduced youtiao—a traditional street-food snack—and other localized dishes at its Chinese locations. Rice bowls also became a staple on Chinese KFC menus.

Thanks to Yum! Brands' realization that there was money in innovating around the Chinese palate, profits from international sales skyrocketed from twenty percent to seventy percent. Setting a measurable goal had cascading consequences for business strategy, product development, marketing, and, ultimately, its overall revenue mix. In the case of Yum! Brands, you definitely get what you measure.

The most powerful type of employee recognition, the kind that shapes culture, occurs informally.

CHAPTER 6

GIVE "WORTHLESS" REWARDS

Worthless rewards are the most valuable rewards.

Recognizing success with innovation is critical, but most companies start and stop with financial incentives. An annual bonus or award is just not enough to catalyze a culture of innovation.

The Most Robust Economy Is a "Recognition Economy"

The most powerful and robust type of recognition—the kind that shapes organizational values—occurs informally. For example, several members of Colgate-Palmolive's global research and development group initiated a "recognition economy" by distributing symbolic wooden nickels to colleagues who had made noteworthy contributions to their projects. The fortunate recipients didn't hoard their winnings. They passed them on to others who had chipped in on projects that they themselves had led. Nickels are now distributed in meetings, but it's not uncommon for employees to return from lunch and find a few nickels anonymously placed on their desks.

The goal is to "formalize" informal rewards. Informal acknowledgments encourage a collective spirit and help promote collaboration and the free flow of ideas. You don't have to dole out wooden nickels to have this type of impact. Just publicly giving credit to others can go a long way in changing people's experiences, reinforcing assumptions, and thus promoting more of the behavior you're giving credit for. A recognition economy based on "conversational credit" can become the basis for dramatically shifting behavior.

Of course, you need to decide what behaviors you want to recognize (such as collaboration, creative problem solving, etc.). And once you've created your short list, you'll likely be able to spot these behaviors more frequently and then recognize them on a more consistent basis. Doing this creates a snowball effect. It's rewarding beyond words to see others begin to give credit to their peers for the things that are most meaningful in driving innovation.

Formal Rewards Should Beckon the Brand

"Worthless" rewards can come in all shapes and sizes. The public television and radio station in San Francisco, KQED, designed an award specifically to reinforce both small and large innovations that surface throughout the year. The award is not about money. KQED designed trophies to recognize their innovators. They're not your ordinary trophies. Atop each stand is the letter *Q* to connect back into the *Q* in KQED. This subtle branding links the award to the organization and to the other innovation efforts happening there, such as the "Q-vation" team, which

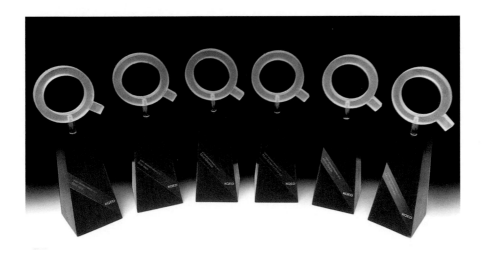

is responsible for collecting ideas and promoting KQED's culture of innovation on an ongoing basis.

Other companies give "experiences" to recognize innovation. Westin, the hotel chain, awards its top innovators a five-day exotic trip each quarter. Sure, there's a financial value to the trip, but Westin's giving away something that's inherent to the service the company provides and to what is being innovated—the travel experience. The award reinforces the value of the customer experience by giving that very experience to those who are most successful in making it better.

Recognize Far and Wide

We've already talked a lot about Intuit, who's established a pretty robust approach to creating a culture of innovation. In the building that sits next to Intuit's corporate office, there's an innovation center that contains Intuit's "Innovation Wall of Fame." Photos and descriptions of individuals and teams are rotated on an annual basis to recognize the innovators who have made the greatest contributions to the business. The wall doesn't honor just those employees who contributed to product innovation. Intuit recognizes all types of innovation across *all* functions, so it's not uncommon to see recognition going to support groups like HR and IT, such as the TechKnow Bar, created by Intuit's IT department so any employee can just walk up and get tech support anytime, just like Apple's Genius Bar.

When it comes to recognition, we can't forget about technology. Recognition can also go virtual, which can spread success stories that both reward the individual and more broadly communicate desired innovation values and behavior. The industrial manufacturing firm Honeywell recognizes innovative contributions each month through its Heroes of the Month award. The recipients of the award are profiled on Honeywell's corporate intranet, which is shared and available to all employees.

While most companies recognize only those who make a direct contribution to technology or product innovation, the best approach involves recognizing anyone who makes a significant contribution, regardless of the type of innovation. Doing so helps spread the value of innovation into areas responsible for the broader operating model. This cultural diffusion happens as a result of highlighting the underlying innovation intent tied to the success story (e.g., this was an HR innovation that transformed how we do college recruiting), which, in turn, reinforces the importance of clearly defining the type of innovation contribution each and every function should be making to the business.

Use Innovation Motivators to Change Culture

So why are "worthless" rewards the most valuable rewards for creating a culture of innovation? Because they go beyond financial incentives to tap into what really motivates people to innovate. It's the deeper motivations—a sense of affiliation, contribution, and making a difference—that can become infectious across an organization and that change culture for the better.

Both formal and informal rewards are founded upon the premise that everything people experience conveys what's important, becomes a symbol of what's valued, and shapes future behavior. Wooden nickels are symbols, trophies are symbols, and a wall of fame is a symbol. The goal is to consciously design your symbols in a way that reinforces your desired innovation intent, so that making innovation a reality becomes everyone's job.

Awesome Example!

NBCUniversal
Growing Talent to Grow the Top Line

Perhaps one of the greatest forms of employee recognition is an investment in someone's personal growth and development. Offering training, and especially identifying someone as "high potential," delivers a plethora of positive signals: You're doing great; you're valued here; we see you going places; we hope you'll be around for a long time to come.

While many companies provide training, few explicitly link professional development to strategic innovation. This practice, however, is the future. Organizations that create a capability at the intersection of professional development and value creation will simultaneously drive a culture of innovation and tangible business growth.

NBCUniversal is doing just that. Widely known for its successful television networks, cable channels, motion pictures, and theme parks,

the company is facing massive change as it navigates a media and entertainment landscape that's being upended by the likes of Netflix, YouTube, Apple, Google, Amazon, BuzzFeed, and a plethora of others. Video games, virtual reality, and homemade videos all now compete for eyeballs and displace television time. Disruption is everywhere.

So, given all this, what is NBCUniversal doing? It's investing in its people—strategically.

Led by Rebecca Romano, Vice President of Talent Development, a small team of learning and development professionals is having a big impact across the company. To start, Rebecca's team created NBCUniversal's Talent Lab. With a presence on both coasts—Los Angeles and New York—it's truly the next generation in creating real value by means of leadership development. The Talent Lab represents the company's new mindset regarding the interplay between talent and innovation and includes a high-tech physical space to match.

The Talent Lab isn't your typical corporate university. The lab includes tiered programs specifically designed for all levels of the organization and for all key phases of employee and professional development—from the company's historic 80-year-old NBCUniversal Page Program for early-career media professionals to programs for senior leaders who are close to transitioning to the executive suite. And it's called a lab because it's just that—a space where people come together, cross-fertilize ideas, and contribute to one another's learning. In addition to facilitating professional development, the lab is a mechanism for materializing NBCUniversal's strategy of fostering "symphony" (i.e., strategic business synergies) across its various businesses and brands.

To promote new mindsets and behaviors that grow the top line, the Talent Lab provides two programs specifically geared to senior leaders whose role it is to shape both culture and business strategy. These two programs aren't about academic case studies. Rather, they focus on high-potential talent—internal talent viewed as game changers, culture carriers, and pioneers for their business. Individuals are recognized by their own management and then invited to participate in one of two programs, DRIVE or CASE on the basis of their current and anticipated strategic roles.

Participants in the Talent Lab's six-month-long DRIVE program comprise twenty-five top executives from across the company's business portfolio. The group is divided into five cohorts, all focused on a specific enterprise business challenge that requires rethinking the company's—and industry's—business model. Cohorts visit parent company Comcast's Silicon Valley incubator, meet with strategic partners, and share

their observations and recommendations with executive management to conclude the program. Along the way, participants gain new mindsets, strategic frameworks, and tools to use in their day jobs running NBC-Universal's various businesses. The result is a one-two punch that includes real opportunities for transforming the industry and a talent base that goes back to "drive" individual businesses with a more strategic lens that is focused on business-model innovation and growth.

The Talent Lab's second program, called CASE, is similar to DRIVE but zeroes in on a specific business case that is facing the company (hence the name CASE). The topic for each CASE program is selected by members of NBCUniversal's executive committee to ensure participants tackle a strategic business issue facing the company at any given time. Topics include things like how to engage millennials by using new forms of entertainment and how to best address emerging multicultural markets that have unique viewing preferences and desires. As with DRIVE, participants break out into teams. But because each case is a bit more granular than the focus of DRIVE, cohorts also engage in ethnographic research with customers and may generate specific ideas for new customer experiences, products, and services. Cohorts return with their specific solutions to the case, which are presented to a panel of strategic leaders for consideration as an enterprise-wide opportunity.

DRIVE and CASE approach professional development from different angles by emphasizing different aspects of value creation and of the innovation process itself. But both programs begin with recognizing those most deserving to participate and then anchoring everything they do in real business needs and opportunities. And both programs deliver deep experiential learning that viscerally infuses innovation not only into participants' views of their own roles but also into their leadership methods, which helps them to collaboratively shape the future of the company, and the industry.

Everything leaders do or say becomes a symbol of what's valued by the organization.

CHAPTER 7

GET SYMBOLIC

Rewrite the unwritten rules.

Everything leadership does communicates what's important and valued in the organization; actions become the symbols that shape culture. As we just discussed, recognition can create the symbols that transmit values. But symbols include much more than just recognition.

Wake Up to Your Unconscious Symbolism

Each and every day, our experiences reinforce specific values, norms, assumptions, and beliefs about what's desired—or undesired—behavior in our organizations. Management and leadership, especially, reinforce these messages in the work environment, as employees typically look to formal authority figures (those who can hire, fire, promote, and allocate resources) to signal what types of behaviors beget promotions, resources, or reprimands. Everything a leader does or says is a symbol of what is good, bad, desired, or undesirable behavior in the organization. So, leaders need to be particularly attuned to what they do and how they do it, whether consciously or unconsciously.

Without awareness of what's being communicated—explicitly and implicitly—values can be reinforced that can either promote or inhibit innovation. One client company of mine, for example, hadn't updated its expense-reporting process in more than twenty years. During that time, the requirements for submitting expenses and receiving reimbursement had devolved into a bureaucratic black hole. Employees with expenses as small and mundane as a client lunch had to undergo an arduous, four-step approval process that could take weeks. Worse still, to receive reimbursements, workers were forced to find time during a ninety-minute window each week when the petty cash department was open. The result? Even though "presume trust" was part of the organization's stated values, many employees didn't feel trusted by management.

This perceived lack of trust had become an innovation barrier for my client. The underlying rhetorical question that stopped many employees in their innovation tracks was this: *If management can't trust me around reimbursement for a ham sandwich, why should I trust them with my good ideas?* (And yes, someone actually said this to me.) The good news is that the company made a simple change to its expense-reporting process (along with other changes), and a big shift in the organization's environment occurred.

The moral of the story? *Little things can have a big impact when it comes to creating a culture of innovation.*

Watch Your Language

I once conducted an innovation-culture assessment for a major food company. As I interviewed its employees, I kept hearing that certain bad ideas were "McCrockers." Huh? Time and time again, I'd hear someone say, "That's a terrible idea. It's a McCrocker!" I soon learned that ten years prior, a food technologist had invented a new cracker and called it a *McCrocker*. It failed miserably in the market. From then on, whenever people wanted to kill an idea, they just called it a *McCrocker!* The moment a new idea was symbolically associated with that painful failure, it became that much harder to get support for moving the idea forward. The company culture had adopted the word *McCrocker* as a symbol of failure and was actively using it to stifle innovation.

Language is a powerful mechanism for shaping culture. Many organizations have their own equivalents of *McCrockers*. Certain words and statements show up frequently across companies and organizations that can easily kill the creative spirit.

The good news is that there's a very simple way to tell if your organization's capacity for innovation is being hampered through language. When you're in meetings look for symbolic language like the following statements that extinguish ideas, sap energy, and gobble up enthusiasm, all in support of the status quo:

- We don't have time to innovate.

- We're not set up for innovation.

- Innovation isn't rewarded.

- We tried that before and it failed.

- We can't do anything until we have more data.

These statements dampen the creative spirit until they kill any possibility of creative invention. While they may be based in historical reality (unfortunately, they usually are), they need to be overcome so a new frame of reference can take hold.

You need to do two things to shift language. First, start to implement some of the culture-changing strategies and programs in this book. You can't expect to change mindsets through just talk—people need to see evidence of new ways of working before they're willing or able to learn a new language.

But as new courses of action that support innovation are being taken, it's also critical to call out the "bad language" when it surfaces and to reframe it, using a future-focused innovation spin. When leaders do this consistently, while pointing out how things are changing for the better, others will start to emulate their behavior. Once people see the verbal molasses that's been reinforcing the status quo culture, they'll want tools for dealing with it themselves. It's leadership's job to tell employees that the next time they hear a verbal wet blanket tossed into the mix, they should throw it back by asking the individual or group questions like these:

- **What's the smallest step** we can take to have the biggest impact, in spite of the identified barrier?

- **What's an example of** a previously successful innovation that spread and grew, despite the perceived barrier? What success factors could be applied again?

- **What have we learned** from previous attempts (failed or otherwise) that we can apply this time around?

- **What can we proactively** do now without permission—and then ask forgiveness for later?

If done right, tactfully challenging "status quo statements" surfaces leadership's commitment to change and provides everyone else with the opportunity to step up and contribute positively to their shared innovation culture. The goal is to put your organization's bad language back in the closet so it stops stamping out fragile ideas.

Rewrite the Unwritten Rules through Curating Cultural Symbols

Symbols represent the unwritten rules of an organization, and they come in many forms—language in the form of catch phrases or acronyms, informal recognition, formal awards, values statements, success stories, posters in the hallways, and even unintended facial expressions. Those who intentionally curate the innovation symbols of their companies essentially curate their innovation cultures.

Intuit's innovation center, for example, features the kitchen table where Scott Cook dreamed up the company with this wife. Employees are encouraged to sit around it for idea jams. Netflix names its corporate conference rooms after blockbuster movies (such as *King Kong*) as a reminder of the continuous breakthroughs its employees are creating and promoting.

Symbols can be more than just physical objects. Poignant stories often live on as folklore that shapes the mindsets and behaviors of new and existing employees. At Google, the story of the time Sheryl Sandberg made a bad decision that cost the company millions lives on—not because of the error itself but because of cofounder Larry Page's response: "I'm so glad you made this mistake," he said, "because I want to run a company where we are moving too quickly and doing too much, not being too cautious and doing too little. If we don't have any of these mistakes, we're just not taking enough risk."

Rather than let stories naturally unfold from leaders' unconscious behavior—which may or may not support innovation—some companies explicitly shape stories to convey key values. The trendy fast-food chain Noodles & Company created a kind of corporate folklore when it invited local marching bands to show up and spontaneously play at nearly one hundred locations around the country. Finding differentiation in the fiercely competitive fast-food field is a tough and ongoing effort, and the story remains a constant reminder that everyone needs to consistently "march to the beat of a different drummer."

In the next two chapters, I'll introduce you to *The Invisible Advantage Culture Questionnaire and Interview Guide* and to the *Invisible Advantage Map* to help you more deeply assess your own culture and figure out what types of symbols may help you jump-start your innovation.

SAP

Shaping the Symbols That Shift Thinking

Perhaps the biggest barrier to creating a culture of innovation is insular thinking—ignoring external trends, emerging technology, and changing customer needs. Insular thinking is inherently inwardly focused. And it's dangerous, since you can be blindsided by threats and miss new opportunities.

Insular thinking is a big challenge for any big company. It's especially humbling for mature companies in a place like Silicon Valley, which are surrounded by faster-moving upstarts who live and breathe an external focus. Such is the case for the software giant SAP.

Tapping into the principles of the "maker movement"—which involves throwing together somewhat random spare parts, tools, and resources to get inspired and experiment—SAP recently created a new experience for employees by creating "d-shops" (short for "developers' workshops").

D-shops are meeting spaces that serve as ad hoc innovation labs where any employee can come, get exposed to a broad range of new technologies, and brainstorm new ideas.

The first d-shop was started at SAP's Palo Alto campus. On the basis of that success, the d-shop was replicated at eleven other locations around the world. D-shops aren't just rooms with movable furniture and whiteboards. Upon entering the d-shop, employees can find and play with the latest in everything cool: 3-D printers, drones, virtual reality headsets, wearables, software, electronic parts, and more.

According to Julien Vayssière, who heads up SAP's d-shop program globally, "We want to encourage people to make time to learn and experiment—to get out of their comfort zone and realize that working with hardware is a lot easier than they think. SAP d-shops remove all barriers that stand in the way of being creative with hardware: We offer workshops at lunchtime, loan the hardware, organize events where colleagues can showcase their projects, or people can just come and mingle with others and create their own demos and prototypes."

The goal is to expose employees at all levels and across all functions to the latest emerging technology, especially technology tied to the Internet of Things, a key strategic focus area for the company. There's no specific innovation goal per se, but "bringing the outside in" helps cross-fertilize existing products with new technology to inspire new thinking and product ideas.

D-shops are symbols that communicate SAP's value for embracing an external perspective, something just about all big companies struggle to do. And in continuing to reinforce the "outside in" theme, SAP did something even more radical. It created HanaHaus, a public café located just outside of its Palo Alto campus.

What? A software company going into the café business? That's right. It's not just any café but an environment that was designed to demonstrate the next generation in collaborative work. At HanaHaus (named after Hana, SAP's latest software platform), anyone can come, sit, and enjoy gourmet coffee and locally made pastries. And anyone can reserve a private workspace or join others in small collaboration rooms. HanaHaus also holds events for skill building and networking. SAP isn't necessary getting into the café business to compete with the likes of Starbucks. It's creating a symbol that clearly communicates the future direction of the company—to bring people together in new ways to shape the future of work.

Both d-shops and HanaHaus are symbols of what's important to the company. They're not necessarily bet-the-farm types of strategies, but they each play a role in demonstrating to employees and the outside world what's valued by SAP—an external focus, experimentation, and emerging technology—which is exactly what SAP sees as essential for creating its future.

Tapping into people's deepest motivations—a sense of affiliation, contribution, and making a difference— is what transforms culture.

CHAPTER 8

ASSESS YOUR INNOVATION CULTURE

Use the Invisible Advantage Questionnaire and Interview Guide
to uncover your innovation culture.

Using online surveys and questionnaires, especially in large organizations, can help you quickly assess your innovation culture.

A word to the wise—surveys tell you only so much. It's also important to take the time to actually speak with real live people. Ask them questions. Interview them. Dig deep to find the root causes of innovation barriers. Get them to talk about innovation success stories that reveal success factors that can be built upon for the future. To help with this process, I provide an interview guide at the end of this chapter.

For now, here is a template that you can use and customize to create your own culture of innovation assessment. This questionnaire is structured using the same categories as the Invisible Advantage Map. Sending it out to a cross section of your organization (or everyone, if that's feasible) can give you a quick yet thorough understanding of your culture. Following this, you can share the survey results and use the map template in a working session with your leadership team to define opportunities for culture change.

Invisible Advantage Questionnaire
Creating a Culture of Innovation

The following things can either enable or inhibit innovation. Please indicate whether you agree or disagree with the following statements. *Your answers should be given on a scale of 1 to 5, where 1 means "strongly disagree" and 5 means "strongly agree."* At the bottom of each section, you have the option to provide any additional thoughts, observations, or recommendations.

1. INNOVATION INTENT

- **Innovation Definition**—My organization has a clear definition of innovation.

  Strongly Disagree ○ Disagree ○ Neutral ○ Agree ○ Strongly Agree ○

- **Innovation Strategies**—My organization focuses on different types of innovation, such as products, services, business models, and business processes.

  Strongly Disagree ○ Disagree ○ Neutral ○ Agree ○ Strongly Agree ○

- **Customer-Focused Innovation**—My organization has specifically outlined what we should be doing to positively improve our customers' lives.

  Strongly Disagree ○ Disagree ○ Neutral ○ Agree ○ Strongly Agree ○

2. LEADERSHIP

- **Leadership Engagement**—
  Leadership is directly involved
  in shaping my organization's
  innovation strategies.

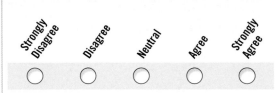

- **Leadership Commitment**—
  Leadership "walks the walk" of
  innovation through role modeling
  and sponsoring specific innovation
  initiatives and projects.

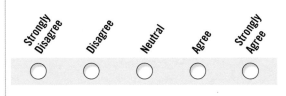

- **Innovation Stories**—Leadership
  consistently shares stories
  about employees, teams, and
  departments that demonstrate
  superior innovation-focused
  values, behaviors, and results.

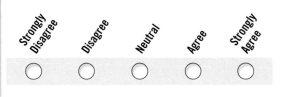

3. STRUCTURE AND PROCESSES

- **Organizational Structure**—My organization has set up a formal structure to oversee innovation, including investments in external opportunities and building internal innovation capabilities.

Strongly Disagree	Disagree	Neutral	Agree	Strongly Agree
○	○	○	○	○

- **Partnerships**—My organization engages external partners and resources in order to tap into new capabilities focused on driving innovation.

Strongly Disagree	Disagree	Neutral	Agree	Strongly Agree
○	○	○	○	○

- **Innovation Process**—My organization has a model and approach that provides guidance on the steps involved in the innovation process.

Strongly Disagree	Disagree	Neutral	Agree	Strongly Agree
○	○	○	○	○

- **Innovation Tools**—My organization has a set of innovation tools appropriate for each step of the innovation process (from identification of "front end" opportunities through the implementation of new ideas).

Strongly Disagree	Disagree	Neutral	Agree	Strongly Agree
○	○	○	○	○

101

4. PEOPLE

- **Recruitment and Selection**—My organization recruits and hires employees who bring a diverse set of innovation-related mindsets and skill sets.

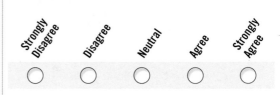

- **Talent Development**—My organization has formal programs designed to develop employee competencies for innovation, including strategic-thinking skills, idea generation, idea prioritization, collaboration, and implementation.

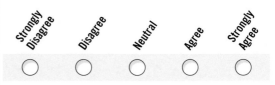

5. REWARDS AND RECOGNITION

- **Rewards**—My organization rewards innovation efforts through formal programs, incentives, or awards.

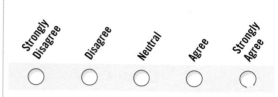

- **Recognition**—Leaders and managers in my organization publicly recognize employees and teams for their innovation accomplishments.

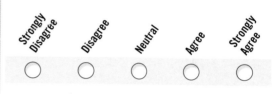

6. INNOVATION METRICS

- **Innovation Metrics**—My organization sets innovation-related goals that are supported by specific measures (e.g., X percent of revenues will come from new products introduced in the last two years).

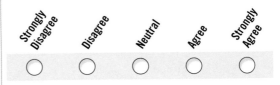

- **Functional Metrics**—The different functions in my organization have established their own individual success metrics related to innovation (however they may define innovation for themselves).

7. ENABLING TECHNOLOGY

- **Innovation-Process Management**—My organization has technology tools for collecting, managing, and developing ideas across the organization.

  Strongly Disagree ○ Disagree ○ Neutral ○ Agree ○ Strongly Agree ○

- **External Collaboration**—My organization uses technology in ways that bring outside knowledge, resources, or partners into the innovation process.

  Strongly Disagree ○ Disagree ○ Neutral ○ Agree ○ Strongly Agree ○

- **Innovation Toolkit**—My organization provides employees and teams with access to a toolbox of models and templates that they can use to help them become more innovative.

  Strongly Disagree ○ Disagree ○ Neutral ○ Agree ○ Strongly Agree ○

Comments: _____

_____

_____

_____

_____

_____

_____

1:1 Interviews—Get Even Deeper Insight

In addition to using the Invisible Advantage Questionnaire, it's also helpful to conduct one-on-one interviews or focus groups with key employees and other stakeholders for a deeper dive into the issues and opportunities. Here are a few questions that I typically use as a starting point (I then add additional questions specifically tailored to the organization):

1. What do you see as your strengths when it comes to innovation?

2. Innovation is clearly important for your future. How do you define *innovation* for the organization overall? How do you define it for your own function in terms of your role and value delivered?

3. What are success stories and examples of times when you or the organization has been especially innovative? Who was involved, what happened, and what were the success factors?

4. Describe your personal vision for how the organization will be operating in three to five years—regarding innovation, what's changed strategically, operationally, and culturally?

5. What do you see as the biggest need and opportunity to build capability to create a true culture of innovation? Consider the following:

   - **Leadership** (vision, communication, sponsorship, cross-functional coordination, etc.)

   - **Organizational structure** (formal organizational structures etc.)

   - **Processes** (within and across functions etc.)

   - **People** (skills, knowledge, experience, etc.)

   - **Metrics** (measure of innovation success etc.)

- **Recognition and rewards** (formal and informal recognition, awards, incentives, etc.)

- **Technology** (internal systems, external tools for gathering customer insights, etc.)

6. If we can make our organization truly world class when it comes to innovation, what does that look like? What is delivered in the short term and then in the longer term?

In the next chapter, I'll review the Invisible Advantage Map, a tool you can use to take this questionnaire and interview data and translate them into an action plan for creating your own culture of innovation.

Creating a culture of innovation isn't about promoting risk taking. It's about eliminating the feeling of "risk" altogether.

CHAPTER 9

DESIGN YOUR INVISIBLE ADVANTAGE

Use the Invisible Advantage Map to create your own invisible advantage.

It's true. *Every organization is perfectly designed to get the results it gets.* Poor performance comes from a poorly designed organization. Superior results emerge when strategies, business models, structure, processes, technologies, tools, and reward systems fire on all cylinders in symphonic unison.

When I work with clients, just about everyone wants to know what, specifically, they can do to promote a culture of innovation, resulting in an invisible competitive advantage that will give them the edge. Said another way, they want to know what levers can be pulled to drive meaningful culture change.

I've created a simple model that anyone can use to better understand—and then design—their innovation culture. The framework includes both big and small levers. Some organizations have strengths in some areas and not others. Other organizations are more challenged and can benefit from looking at all dimensions.

The Invisible Advantage Map is a simple tool that can help guide and facilitate strategy and organizational design sessions. Here's the template:

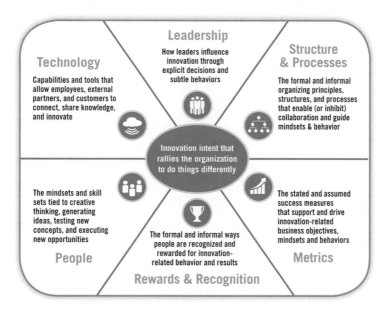

Companies like Intuit have created cultures that have artfully integrated aspects of each of these areas. They take a holistic view of their cultures, ensuring that leadership reinforces the specific structures, processes, metrics, rewards, and talents required for sustaining innovation.

Here's an examples of Intuit's Invisible Advantage Map:

To get you started with your own version, I've created an initial list of things that could go into the Invisible Advantage Map for each of the areas. Remember, every organization and culture is different, so what's relevant and appropriate will vary from one context to the next.

LEADERSHIP

- Define an innovation portfolio (small, medium, and big opportunities).

- Create small teams.

- Promote rapid prototyping.

- Promote experimentation.

- Tell innovation stories.

- Identify and overcome "wet blankets."

STRUCTURE AND PROCESSES

- Create an innovation council to oversee innovation strategy and investments.

- Create an innovation lab.

- Build cross-functional innovation teams.

- Design and implement an innovation process.

- Build an "open innovation" process to get external ideas.

- Create a "customer office hours" process that allows employees to interact with customers each month.

- Implement monthly "brown bag" sessions in which external speakers share new ideas.

- Bring employees together in "poster sessions" to share and learn about projects.

- Conduct "idea competitions" for collecting ideas from employees, partners, and customers.

PEOPLE

- Recruit people with mindsets and skill sets tied to innovation.

- Provide innovation training.

- Give people free time to experiment on pet projects.

- Surprise people with "boomerang passes" (see Chapter 3).

- Promote networking lunches to help people across functions meet one another.

- Create open meeting spaces where people can spontaneously meet and network.

METRICS

- Define a portfolio of metrics related to the organization's leadership, employees, and customers (the following are a few examples from Chapter 5).

  › Percentage of funding for game changers versus small tweaks to existing products or services

  › Percentage of senior executive time focused on the future versus on daily operations

  › Percentage of new innovations that come from external sources, such as partnerships, crowdsourcing, or open innovation

  › Number of ideas turned into innovation experiments by employees

  › Number of teams that submit projects for innovation awards

  › Percentage of employees trained in the innovation process

  › Number of customers that help test and refine new ideas

REWARDS AND RECOGNITION

○ Provide individual, team, department, business unit, and/or company-wide awards.

○ Create quarterly innovation awards.

○ Create annual innovation awards.

○ Give free time as an award.

○ Give gift cards as an award.

○ Create an innovation "wall of fame" to highlight success stories.

○ Share success stories on the corporate intranet.

○ Share success stories in the company newsletter.

○ Share success stories in monthly, quarterly, and annual meetings.

○ Give people who rise up as role models new positions to promote innovation or work on innovation teams (permanent or rotating positions).

TECHNOLOGY

○ Implement an idea-management system for collecting, evaluating, and executing ideas from employees.

○ Utilize online, mobile, and hard copy toolkits with innovation models and templates.

○ Create Internet and intranet sites for sharing tools, resources, and stories.

○ Develop or join an external "open innovation" platform for gathering ideas from customers and partners.

When you use the Invisible Advantage Map and start brainstorming, think about the things you can do within each area to create a system of reinforcing structures, processes, metrics, rewards, and tools to give people the mindsets and skill sets they need in order to innovate in your organizational context. And remember to focus on leadership—this is what gives your plans real legs. Leaders must practice what they preach on the map, and they must do those critical few things outlined in the previous chapters. Unless you've committed to taking these essential measures, don't even bother brainstorming.

Leading innovation requires innovating how you lead.

CHAPTER 10

GET GOING IN
FOUR SIMPLE STEPS

Calling all facilitators, consultants, and change agents . . .
Use the Invisible Advantage Toolkit to get started now!

Although there isn't a set formula for creating a culture of innovation per se, there are principles and practices that you can use to understand your current culture, define the values and behaviors you want, and do things to get it.

I've made the best of the best resources—all downloadable free of charge—available to complement this book because I believe infusing innovation into an organization's culture enhances the quality of work life, creates value for customers, and ultimately makes the world a better place. Simple as that. You can download the entire Invisible Advantage Toolkit and other resources at **www.innovation-point.com/toolkit**.

And if you're leading a strategy- or culture-change project in your organization, here are four simple steps you can take, using the Toolkit to jump-start your process:

1. Assemble your leadership team and agree that creating a culture of innovation is a strategic imperative. As part of the process, use the video *The Invisible Advantage* to communicate the need and opportunity.

2. Use the Invisible Advantage Questionnaire and Interview Guide to conduct an innovation-culture assessment.

3. Reconvene your leadership team and review your findings. Use the Invisible Advantage Map as a framework for brainstorming potential solutions to challenges and opportunities.

4. Create an action plan that ensures that leadership "walks the walk" by taking the steps outlined in the previous chapters and completing anything else that you added to your own version of the Invisible Advantage Map.

Of course, you have to implement and stay on top of that action plan through regular check-ins, reassessment of your culture, and so on.

Most leaders and organizations today want innovation, especially the game changers. And there's no shortage of resources out there. But perhaps the most important secret to sustainable innovation has been staring us in the face all along.

Instead of new tools, templates, and processes, we need new assumptions and mindsets. The primary role of leadership is fostering just the right environment for individuals and teams to flourish. That's what creating a real culture of innovation is all about. And that's what will produce your invisible advantage.

ABOUT THE AUTHOR

SOREN KAPLAN is the author of the best-selling and award-winning books *Leapfrogging* and *The Invisible Advantage*, an affiliated professor at the Center for Effective Organizations at USC's Marshall School of Business, a writer for *Fast Company*, a globally recognized keynote speaker, and the founder of InnovationPoint. As a leading expert in disruptive innovation, innovation culture, and strategic change, he works with Disney, NBCUniversal, Kimberly-Clark, Colgate-Palmolive, Hershey, Red Bull, Medtronic, Roche, Philips, Cisco,

Visa, Ascension Health, Kaiser Permanente, American Nurses Association, CSAA Insurance Group, and numerous other organizations. Soren previously led the internal strategy and innovation group at Hewlett-Packard (HP) during the roaring 1990s in Silicon Valley and was a cofounder of iCohere, one of the first web collaboration platforms for online learning and social networking. He has lectured at the Harvard Business School, Copenhagen Business School, Melbourne Business School, and with other MBA and executive-education programs. He has been quoted, published, and interviewed by *Fast Company*, *Forbes*, *CNBC*, *National Public Radio*, the *American Management Association*, *USA Today*, *Strategy & Leadership*, and *The International Handbook on Innovation*, among many others. He holds Master's and PhD degrees in Organizational Psychology, resides in the San Francisco Bay Area, and possesses dual US-French citizenship.

Get the FREE Toolkit

Good news! A free toolkit that contains download-able digital versions of *The Invisible Advantage* video, Invisible Advantage questionnaire, Invisible Advantage interview guide, Invisible Advantage Map PowerPoint template, and Invisible Advantage Map large format poster, is available at:

www.innovation-point.com/toolkit

Learn More

The author is the founder of InnovationPoint®, a global think tank and consultancy that serves the most innovative Fortune 500 companies and is a leader in growth strategy, innovation culture, and leadership development.

InnovationPoint offers free resources including articles, white papers, innovation culture assessments, book chapters, and more at:

www.innovation-point.com/resources

If you are looking for more information about how to bring these tools into your own organization, or for support in teaching others how to create a culture of innovation, contact us at:

1-925-405-5003 or visit
www.innovation-point.com

Innovation Keynotes

Have Soren Kaplan or one of his colleagues, who are experts in innovation growth strategy, innovation culture, and leadership, jump start your next event or conference by delivering a dynamic presentation that will inspire a change in—and commitment to—creating your Invisible Advantage.

For more information, visit:

www.leapfrogging.com

or email inquiry@leapfrogging.com for speaking rates and availability.